Contents

Off to Italy!

We are going on holiday to Italy. This is a country in the south of Europe. It is shaped like a high-heeled boot.

Two large islands are part of Italy too. They are called Sicily and Sardinia. You can see them on the map.

We are visiting in summer so it will be hot. But it might still be cool in the evenings or when we visit the mountains.

Here are some things I know about Italy...

- Foods that originally came from Italy, such as pizza and pasta, are eaten all over the world today.

- Many famous artists, such as Michaelangelo and Leonardo da Vinci, came from Italy. Their art is displayed all over the world.

- Italy is a peninsula. It sticks out into the Mediterranean Sea and is surrounded by water on three sides.

On our trip I'm going to find out lots more!

Arriving in Milan.

We arrive in Milan in the afternoon. Outside the airport the air is hot and sticky.

Milan is a big city in the north of Italy. Many people live and work here. Every year big fashion shows are held here in the spring and autumn.

For my first meal in Italy I have **risotto**. It is like a savoury rice pudding with herbs and mushrooms. It is lovely and creamy.

After lunch we go to see the *Duomo*. This is an enormous cathedral. You can go up and walk on the roof. The view is amazing. The guide book says that on a clear day you can see a range of mountains called the Alps.

The *Duomo* is the largest Gothic cathedral in the world. It took five hundred years to build.

mountains and lakes

From Milan we travel by train to Lake Garda.

First, we have windsurfing lessons on the lake. It is lots of fun, but the water is cold when we fall in.

Our instructor says this is the largest lake in Italy. At the south it is wide and the land is flat. To the north the lake is narrower and surrounded by craggy mountains.

The next day we go hiking in the Dolomites. This is the name for the eastern part of the Alps.

The highest parts of the mountains are jagged and rocky. Lower down there are lots of wild flowers and bright green grass. In the winter these slopes are covered with snow and people ski here.

Golden eagle

The area we are in is a national park. These are areas where wild animals and their **habitats** are protected.

9

The floating city

From the Dolomites we travel east all the way to the sea at Venice.

Vaporetto

Dad says that Venice is built on 117 islands that are separated by canals. Everyone in Venice travels by water. We take a water-bus called a *vaporetto* down the Grand Canal to the *Piazza San Marco.*

The piazza is the main square. It is in front of the church of Saint Mark, or the *Basilica di San Marco*. This is one of the most famous places in Venice and is very crowded with people.

In the narrow streets around the piazza, people sell carnival masks and Venetian glass.

Venice is a very old city. For hundreds of years it was an important port for people trading between Europe and eastern countries, such as China and India.

Fabulous Florence

Today we take the train from Venice to Florence. On the way we cross the River Po.

This river brings water to the surrounding land, which makes this area good for farming. Crops, such as wheat and rice, are grown here.

To get to the city centre from our hotel we have to cross the *Ponte Vecchio*. This is an old bridge over the River Arno. There are jewellery shops all along the sides of the bridge.

Ponte Vecchio

We walk on to find the *Palazzo Vecchio*. This is Florence's town hall. It looks more like a castle to me.

On the way we stop at a *gelateria*. This is an ice cream shop. The ice cream is made right there in the shop. There are all sorts of flavours to choose from. I choose the bright green pistachio ice cream. Yum!

Before leaving Florence we go to the Uffizi art gallery. We have to queue for ages, but it's worth it. Many famous artists have lived and worked in Florence. There are 45 rooms full of art at the Uffizi, so it takes a long time to look around.

In the afternoon we hire a car and drive up into the hills. Mum has found a villa where we can stay. It has stone walls and an orange tiled roof.

We are in the region of Tuscany. The hills are green and there are rows of thin trees that Dad says are called cypress trees. There are vineyards with grape vines planted in rows, and olive trees with their silvery leaves.

After two days here we set off for Rome.

Exploring the capital

Rome is Italy's capital city. Lots of people come to visit the city each year. There are old buildings that have been here for a long time, and new, modern buildings.

When we get to the centre it is busy and noisy. Drivers are beeping their horns at each other and there are scooters whizzing about. A policeman blows his whistle very loudly to direct the traffic.

There are lots of sights to see in Rome. My favourite is the Trevi fountain. In the centre is the sea god, Neptune, and on either side are horses that are pulling his chariot in the sea.

In the evening we go to a restaurant. It is busy and lots of people are eating and laughing together. We eat pasta, shaped like ribbons, in tomato sauce. It is delicious.

The Eternal City

Rome is known as the 'Eternal City' because it is so old. More than two thousand years ago people called the Romans ruled a great empire, and Rome was its centre.

The Colosseum

Many buildings that the Romans built are still standing today. One is the Colosseum. It is an enormous oval arena. Romans would watch entertainments here, such as **gladiator** fights.

On our last day in Rome we go to Vatican City. This is where the Pope lives. He is head of the Roman Catholic Church. Most people in Italy are Catholics.

There is a wall around Vatican City that separates it from the rest of Rome. This is because it is a different country and even has its own postal service and army (below).

Next stop ... Naples

I am looking forward to going to Naples as my teacher told me that this is where pizza was invented. At the *pizzeria* they have a **wood-burning oven** for cooking the pizzas.
My pizza has tomatoes, olives, ham and cheese on.
Yum!

Near Naples is a huge volcano called Mount Vesuvius. We walk up to see the big crater at the top. On the way we pass more olive trees and vines.

Mount Vesuvius

A preserved city

In 79 BCE Mount Vesuvius erupted. The lava and hot ash from the eruption covered the cities of Herculaneum and Pompeii.

Many hundreds of years later scientists discovered that the city of Pompeii was still there under the rock. Since then, they have uncovered the remains of the ancient city.

The Amalfi Coast

Next we travel south to the Amalfi Coast. We are staying in a hotel near the small town of Amalfi.

The road winds back and forth. On one side is a high cliff and on the other the land drops steeply into the sea. The drive is quite scary.

The hotel owner is called Catarina. Her family live nearby and help her to run the hotel. I took this photo of some of them.

Catarina's eldest daughter, Bianca, goes to school in Amalfi. She has to get up early because lessons start at 8.30am, but she finishes at 2.00pm. In the afternoon she helps her Mum or goes to the beach.

At the market

For a few days we are going to travel around southern Italy. This is a big region but there are fewer cities than in the north.

At one town we go to a bustling market. All the stalls are selling different foods. Mum says that they have all been grown or made nearby.

There are lots of types of bread and cakes. Fruit stalls are piled high with oranges and lemons. There are bright red tomatoes and purple aubergines.

At the cheese stall a man gives us some cheese to taste. Nearby, a woman is selling olive oil.

Over the sea to Sicily

When we get to the city of Reggio di Calabria we are right at the toe of the boot of Italy. We get on a ferry to cross the Straits of Messina to Sicily.

We are going to take the train from Messina to the island's capital city, Palermo.

Did you know that Sicily was once part of Greece? You can still see Greek temples near the city of Agrigento.

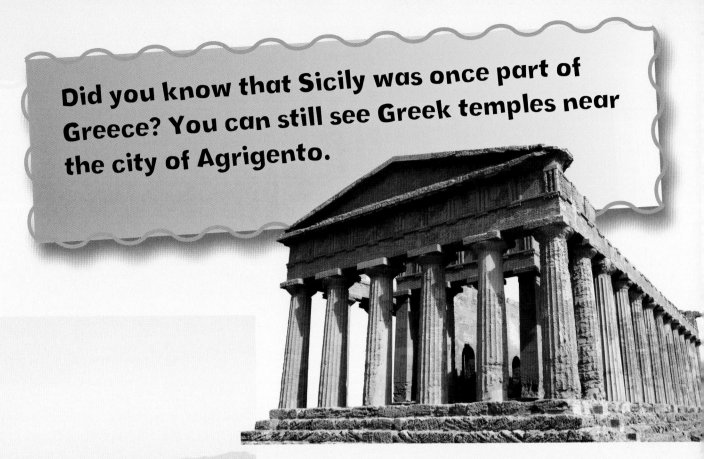

The railway runs along the Tyrrhenian coast. The sea is bright blue and there are lots of small, rocky coves and misty islands.

In Palermo we go to a little street cafe. Sicily is famous for cakes and puddings. We try *cannoli*. These are pastries, stuffed with **ricotta** cheese and covered with chocolate. Fantastic!

Sparkling Sardinia

Sardinia is the final place we are going to visit. There is one boat a week from Palermo to Cagliari, Sardinia's capital city. The journey takes thirteen hours.

In the city there are lots of old buildings as well as new ones. We climb up inside an old tower called the *Torre San Pacrizo*. From the top we can see the old town and the port. People look very small and busy from up here.

On the north-east coast of Sardinia is an area called *La Costa Smeralda*, or 'the emerald coast'. This is a popular holiday place for wealthy people.

Before we leave we travel inland to see the *nuraghi*. These buildings were built when the **indigenous** people of Sardinia lived here between 1500 and 500 BCE.

From Cagliari we travel back to Milan to catch our flight home. I can't wait to tell my friends about our trip to Italy!

My first words in Italian

Buon giorno (*say* **Bwohn-johrnoh**)	Hello
Arrivederci (*say* **Ahrryvehdehrchy**)	Goodbye
Come stai? (*say* **Kohmeh stahy**)	How are you?
Come ti chiami? (*say* **Kohmeh tyh kyahmy**)	What is your name?
Mi chiamo Sandra. (*say* **Myh kyahmoh Sandra**)	My name is Sandra.

Counting 1-10

1 **uno**   2 **due**   3 **tre**   4 **quattro**

5 **cinque**   6 **sei**   7 **sette**   8 **otto**

9 **nove**   10 **dieci**

Words to remember

gladiator a person in ancient Rome who fought other people or animals to entertain an audience

Gothic a style of architecture

habitat the place where an animal lives

indigenous originating from, or native to, a particular country or region

peninsula a strip of land that is almost completely surrounded by sea

ricotta a soft, white cheese made with sheep's milk

risotto a thick rice dish, with meat, fish, seafood or vegetables added

wood-burning oven an oven that uses wood for fuel

Index

Learning more about Italy

Books

Italy (Looking at Countries) Jillian Powell, Franklin Watts, 2006.
Italy (The Changing Face of) Kathryn Britton, Wayland, 2007.
Italy (Young Explorer: We're from) Vicky Parker, Heinemann Library, 2006.
What's it like to live in Italy? Jillian Powell, Wayland, 2003.

Websites

National Geographic Kids, People and places
  http://kids.nationalgeographic.com/places/find/italy
Geography for kids, Geography online and Geography games
  http://www.kidsgeo.com/index.php
SuperKids Geography directory, lots of sites to help with geography learning.
  http://www.super-kids.com/geography.html